THE
TRINITY
IS THE
MATRIX

The Grand Unified Theory of Everything That Blends
Faith with Science to Prove the Existence of God

GARY D. COMBS

WESTBOW
PRESS®
A DIVISION OF THOMAS NELSON
& ZONDERVAN

WestBow Press books may be ordered through booksellers or by contacting:

WestBow Press
A Division of Thomas Nelson & Zondervan
1663 Liberty Drive
Bloomington, IN 47403
www.westbowpress.com
844-714-3454

Scripture taken from the King James Version of the Bible.

ISBN: 978-1-6642-3046-0 (sc)
ISBN: 978-1-6642-3045-3 (e)

Print information available on the last page.

WestBow Press rev. date: 04/06/2021

All science is essentially
a search for unity.
—Paul Davies

To my mom, dad, and brother.

CONTENTS

PREFACE

Solved are two great mysteries: science's search to understand the grand unified theory of everything, and Christianity's search to understand the Lord's omnipresent nature, both of which are the exact same thing—only clothed in different terminology.

Thus the big bang theory and the theory of evolution are both biblical principles as first recorded in the Genesis account of creation written by Moses some 3,500 years ago.

INTRODUCTION:
MONOCLES AND GLASSES

The greatest enemy of knowledge is not ignorance, it's
the illusion of knowledge.

—Stephen Hawking

If our Creator exists as omnipresent, as widely believed, then what is His physical body made from that empowers Him to exist hidden from us in plain sight?

Mindful of that question, theologians have long sought to understand the mystery of the Lord's omnipresent nature, while scientists have long sought to understand the grand unified theory of everything. Unbeknownst to them, each holds the key to the other's understanding. Christianity reveals the nature of the Godhead's three-part character, and science reveals the nature of His three-part physical being, each of which exists as the exact same thing, only clothed in different terminology.

This concept of one substance that simultaneously exists as three separate and distinct forms is known as a state of three-in-one singularity, with our best example being H_2O. After all, H_2O simultaneously exists as water, ice, and vapor, each of which is the exact same thing (H_2O) in a distinct form. Completely interchangeable.

In fact, it's common knowledge that the three states of matter are liquid, solid, and gas; therefore, with H_2O as a type of matter, water is liquid, ice is solid, and vapor is gas. The Trinity, as a three-in-one singularity, could be likened to the three states of matter as well, with the Father being the more liquid, the Son being the more solid, and the Holy Spirit being the more vaporous, though as yet you know not how.

First, science has long sought to understand how our universe could have manifested itself from nothing, while virtually all religions have sought to understand how our Creator could have manifested Himself from nothing as well.

Second, know that Christianity has long proclaimed our God to be one God who simultaneously exists in three separate and distinct "bodies," commonly referred to as "persons," a.k.a. the Trinity. This means that God Almighty is one God who simultaneously exists in three separate and distinct forms—meaning three-in-one singularity—with each body/person being the exact same thing in a different form. Completely interchangeable.

With those things said, when considering how to understand the nature of God's physical being, let's begin with the obvious. To the human eye, God Almighty exists as invisible and intangible yet mysteriously hidden from us in plain sight as omnipresent.

That description now leads us to reason that if we can find something in our universe that exists as invisible and intangible yet also mysteriously hides from us in plain sight as omnipresent, then it's highly likely we've discovered how to perceive God's physical being.

Amazingly, there is something we're all familiar with that meets that description: the realm of subatomic building blocks from which all things are created.

Yes. Our subatomic realm and the Trinity are invisible and intangible yet mysteriously hidden from us in plain sight as omnipresent;

however, in and of itself, that description isn't enough to satisfy our need.

Simply put, what we must discover is just what exactly our subatomic realm is comprised of, because that substance exists as the conjunction that joins our subatomic realm and the Trinity into a common entity. Therefore, if our subatomic realm were to be created from one substance that exists in a state of three-in-one singularity, as does the Trinity, then we'd be able to understand how to link them together as one common and eternal entity.

Amazingly, there is such a substance, and to my knowledge, that substance was first recorded in Professor Paul Davies's 1984 book *Superforce*. But, to my knowledge at least, no one has yet been able to discern how that superforce substance is able to exist in a state of three-in-one singularity and, in turn, becomes the conjunction that links our subatomic realm and the Trinity together as one entity from which the totality of our universe is comprised—thus making our three-part subatomic realm the nature of the Godhead's physical being, with the Trinity being the nature of the Godhead's character.

All of which now leads us to *autostereograms*.

Back in the early 1990s, autostereograms became quite popular in the United States, being computer-generated three-dimensional pictures of repeated patterns that camouflage images from view—being hidden in plain sight.

Everyone could easily see those repeated patterns, though not everyone could see the hidden images within them, as those hidden images had been camouflaged by their patterns. In other words, the visible patterns camouflaged the hidden images within them.

So too is the Lord's omnipresent nature singular with the world's patterns around us, as His invisible, intangible, physical presence has been camouflaged by visible, tangible trees, buildings, clouds, and everything else that we can see. But this is only because our ignorance and illusions of knowledge have prevented our minds from having our "lights turned on."

Before that can happen, however, we must form the necessary perspectives to enlighten our blind spots and empower us to perceive—we must have our "lights turned on."

Our first blind spot exists due to our division of sight, meaning monocles, because for far too long we've sought to discover our answers through our single-eye sight. Meaning that Christianity has long sought to understand the mystery of the Lord's omnipresent nature through its monocle of biblical understanding, while science has long sought to understand the mystery of the grand unified theory of everything through its monocle of scientific understanding.

What both sides fail to appreciate is that the other holds its key of understanding; therefore, spiritual glasses of newfound perceptions are needed in order to see through both eyes simultaneously. After all, we're born with two eyes. That doesn't mean that each eye looks at two different things, but rather they look at the exact same thing from two slightly different angles to empower us with the clarity of sight.

Mindful of that, some of us are farsighted while others of us are nearsighted. Some are right-eye dominant while others are left-eye dominant; regardless, prescription glasses are needed in order to properly balance our sight for the restoration of our visual clarity.

As is the natural realm, so, too, is the spiritual realm. Those who are right-eye dominant have little to do with faith, some being atheists, because they're only willing to look through their dominant monocle of scientific understanding. Conversely, those who are left-eye dominant have little to do with science—some wrongly believing doctors and scientists to be the enemies of faith because they're only willing to look through their dominant monocle of religious understanding.

If either one ever took the time to form the new perceptions of spiritual glasses needed to simultaneously see through both eyes, then they'd discover that our right eye of science better reveals *how* the Lord created and maintains our universe, while our left eye of faith better reveals *why*.

In so doing, scientists would learn to incorporate Christianity into their grand unified theory of everything, because by nature Christianity is a part of everything; conversely, Christians would come to discover that scientists and doctors are good things. After all, Luke was a physician who wrote two books of the Bible, while the Good Samaritan who performed medical services on the injured man was called "the Good Samaritan," not the faithless, unbelieving one.

I'm reminded of a story in which some rock star spoke with a wannabe guitarist who always practiced the same songs over and over again. The wannabe sought to ensure he always played those songs perfectly.

The rock star said, "If you don't make mistakes when you practice, then you're practicing the wrong things."

Physicists and theologians alike have sought to accumulate in the same areas of knowledge for so long that they've been practicing the wrong things. They've sought to continuously strengthen their dominant eye of understanding at the expense of their weaker eye; conversely, they should have conducted themselves more like professional bodybuilders. After all, professional bodybuilders never curl weights with just their dominant arm, as it would grow strong and bulky while their weaker arm remained weak and thin—oddly out of balance.

Yet that's exactly what most theologians and scientists have done—continuously fed their dominant eye until it's become oddly out of balance with the weaker eye, which has blinded them from seeing their desired answers.

Along with that, I'm reminded of an old adage about a man who lost his car keys one night. As fate would have it, his car was parked by a streetlight, and the man searched for hours in vain under that streetlight for his keys. For whatever reason, it never occurred to him that although the light was there, that didn't mean his keys were, and his keys must be hidden somewhere in the darkness.

Similarly, for countless centuries theologians and scientists have separately sought in vain to discover their missing insights of knowledge that would empower them to perceive the answers to the mysteries that they've long sought to understand. As each of them have continuously sought their answers through their monocle of "streetlight understanding," they've never realized that their answers can only be found under the streetlight of the other's understanding.

And there it is: monocles versus glasses. For far too long we've sought our answers through our single-eyed sight of arrogant monocles, as opposed to our double-eyed sight of humble glasses, meaning we must admit that the other side is right as well.

In so doing, Christians must understand that scientific laws, not theories, are perfect in their assertions, while nonbelievers must understand that the Bible is also perfect in its assertions as well, though the Bible's clouds of figurative terminology can be difficult to interpret. This in turn reveals that Christianity and science are not two different subjects but rather the exact same subject as studied and taught from two different points-of-view, as Christianity better reveals the nature of the Godhead's character, while science better reveals the nature of the Godhead's physical being.

The newfound perceptions empower us to forsake our monocles of understanding for the glasses which empower our weaker eye to clearly see in focus, and in turn allow our "light to be turned on" in order to perceive our desired insights that show forth from the autostereogram which surrounds us.

Mindful of all these things, this writing is structured around the King James six-day account of creation.

Contrary to traditional Christian theology, those six days were not literally six twenty-four-hour days, but rather six stages of creation that occurred in varying timeframes, figuratively referred to as days. Thus the sentence "And the evening and the morning were the first day" doesn't literally refer to a sunrise and sunset, but figuratively stands as a curtain to open and close each act of our life's play.

For at least three different reasons we know that to be true.

First, on day three the Lord created the Earth's land, water, and plant life, while traditional Christian theology teaches our sun and moon were created on day four as the greater light to rule the day and the lesser light to rule the night.

Common sense dictates that cannot be true. The Lord couldn't have made the Earth's plant life prior to the creation of the sun and moon simply because the plant life would have lacked the heat and photosynthesis needed to sustain it.

Second, on day six the Lord commanded Adam and Eve to replenish the earth, meaning to replace what previously existed on day five. If those six days of creation were literally twenty-four-hour days, as many believe, then Adam and Eve had to replenish what the Lord had just created and then suddenly destroyed, not twenty-four hours prior.

Obviously, that doesn't make any sense.

Some fundamental Christians site the gap theory, which I've detailed in the day six chapter, in an attempt to reconcile that discrepancy.

Realize also that a paradox is created whenever a scientific law, not theory, seemingly contradicts scripture, making it our responsibility to revise our interpretations until the scientific law and scriptures agree. In so doing, we'll become more like our wiser scientific brethren who've mastered the art of formulating theories void of arrogance, as scientific theories are written with the express intention of having others revise them into law.

Following these reasonings, flexibility is perhaps the single greatest strength of a scientific theory, as its lack of arrogance paves the way for future revisions that will promote it into law. Unfortunately, flexibility is a quality that many in the church despise because they want perfection from the outset, using any imperfection in any theory to reaffirm their confidence in scripture's infallibility.

In other words, they want the fullness of light all at once, as opposed to allowing their light to progressively grow brighter and brighter through revised studies. Similarly, Luke 19:11 reveals that many Israelites also made that same illusion-of-knowledge mistake when they failed to receive Jesus as their Messiah "because they thought that the kingdom of God should immediately appear."

Regardless, if we're faithful to do these things, then, in time, we'll develop our new perception glasses that will convert our sight from our two eyes of division and into a more unified state of clarity, making the mysteries of our existence understandable.

Unexpectedly, those mysteries become irrelevant, as a new reality sets in.

The invisible intangible and camouflaged presence of God Almighty suddenly shows forth as separate, yet one with His visible, tangible, autostereogram form, never again to be hidden from us in plain sight.

It's exhilarating!

The Intangible Universe

One of the things I like about doing science, that is the most fun, is coming up with something that seems ridiculous when you first hear it, but finally seems obvious when you've finished.

—Fisher Black

As a three-in-one substance, the superforce of our subatomic realm exists in these three separate and distinct forms:

1. The four known fundamental forces of nature.
2. Elementary particles in all their forms.
3. The light of the laws of knowledge.

When joining the superforce's three-in-one physical nature to our spiritual three-in-one God, we can perceive that:

- God the Holy Spirit physically exists as the four known fundamental forces of nature, being omnipotent, as nothing is more powerful than energy in all its forms.

- God the Son physically exists as elementary particles in all their forms, being omnipresent, as nothing is more ever-present than the totality of elementary particles.
- God the Father physically exists as the light of the laws of knowledge, being omniscience, as nothing is more all-knowing than the laws of knowledge.

For proof of this assertion, consider these three scientific laws:

1. The law of conservation of quantum information states that quantum information can be neither created nor destroyed, only hidden from us.[1]

    Just as quantum information cannot be created or destroyed, only hidden from us, neither can God the Father be created or destroyed. Or, as Deuteronomy 29:29 (NIV) reads, "The secret things belong to the Lord our God, but the things revealed belong to us and to our children forever."

    The laws of knowledge are probably contained within the Higgs Field, and/or Higgs boson, as energy and elementary particles in all their forms are forced to flow through and operate in accordance with it.

2. The law of conservation of mass states that matter (elementary particles) can neither be created nor destroyed.[2]

    Just as matter cannot be created or destroyed, neither can God the Son be created or destroyed.

---

[1] Wikipedia, s.v. last edited February 23, 2021, https://en.wikipedia.org/wiki/No-hiding_theorem

[2] National Geographic Society, "The Conservation of Matter during Physical and Chemical Changes," National Geographic, January 13, 2020, https://www.nationalgeographic.org/article/conservation-matter-during-physical-and-chemical-changes/6th-grade/.

3. The law of conservation of energy states that energy can neither be created nor destroyed, but merely changes form.[3]

   Just as energy cannot be created or destroyed, but merely changes form, neither can God the Holy Spirit be created or destroyed. He simply changes form as well.

Notice that neither of those properties can be created or destroyed, which implies they must be the exact same thing in a different form, thus existing in a three-in-one state of singularity, just like H_2O or the Trinity.

To give a little history on the superforce, in the 1920s a Belgian priest named Georges Lemaître was the first to theorize the big bang origins of our universe through the expansion of a primordial atom. Then, in 1984, Professor Paul Davies' book *Superforce* described that big bang primordial atom as being the four known fundamental forces of nature being tightly held together into one superforce.

At the time of the big bang, "One by one the four fundamental forces separated out from the superforce. Step by step the particles which go to build all the matter in the world acquired their present identities."[4]

In describing the effects of this superforce, Professor Davies stated,

> Together these investigations point towards a compelling idea, that all nature is ultimately controlled by the activities of a single *superforce*. The superforce would have the power to bring the universe into being and to furnish it with light, energy, matter, and structure. But the superforce would amount to more

---

[3] University of Calgary, "Law of Conservation of Energy," energyeducation.ca, last updated April 28, 2020, https://energyeducation.ca/encyclopedia/Law_of_conservation_of_energy#:~:text=The%20law%20of%20conservation%20of,it's%20added%20from%20the%20outside.

[4] Paul Davies, *Superforce* (New York: Simon and Schuster, 1984), 8.

> than just a creative agency. It would represent an amalgamation of matter, spacetime, and force into an integrated and harmonious framework that bestows upon the universe a hitherto unsuspected unity.[5]

Along with that he also said, "If we unlock this superforce it would give us power beyond all imagination. It might even explain how the universe came to exist in the first place."[6]

This means that at the beginning of time the only thing in existence was God Almighty in His superforce physical form of the four known fundamental forces of nature all tightly compacted together, surrounded by utter nothingness; the release of that big bang superforce of energy empowered the tiny beginning of our universe to expand into that void of nothingness.

Regardless of that, what we want to know is, how did everything manifest itself from nothing?

Actually this becomes quite simple to explain through the use of a new perception.

First of all, forsake the concept of everything manifesting itself from nothing, as the word *appeared* is more appropriate than the word *manifested*.

What I mean is that only one form, being the four fundamental forces of nature, had manifested itself from nothing, which is what our scientific community refers to as the big bang's superforce, while the other two forms, being elementary particles and the light of the laws of knowledge, merely appeared later as a result of the big bang's cooling temperature.

---

[5] Davies, *Superforce*, 5–6, italics in original.
[6] Davies, *Superforce*, 21.

This is similar to how water is first present, then later appears as ice or vapor, with our very best example being snowflakes. After all, snowflakes do not manifest themselves out of nothing but rather from the air's moisture as it freezes. That is, the air's moisture and snowflakes are both the exact same thing in a different form. Completely interchangeable.

In like manner, that's exactly what happened during the early stages of our universe's formation. Sometime after the big bang's superforce release of energy began to cool, elementary particles in all their different forms began to appear, just like snowflakes begin to appear when the air's moisture begins to freeze. Along with that, just as snowflakes are completely interchangeable with the air's moisture, so too are elementary particles completely interchangeable with the four known fundamental forces of nature.

Therefore, just as snowflakes "clump" together to form snowballs and even larger snowmen, so too can elementary particles be "clumped" together to form atoms, molecules, mineral dust, stars, and planets.

The CERN website best explains this by saying, "In the first moments after the Big Bang, the universe was extremely hot and dense. *As the universe cooled, conditions became just right to give rise to the building blocks of matter—the quarks and electrons of which we are all made*"[7] (italics added).

Notice, elementary particles weren't created, per se, but rather appeared in our universe when their original state of energy began to cool—just like snowflakes do.

Similarly, Professor Brian Koberlein wrote, "Albert Einstein's most famous equation says that energy and matter are two sides of the

---

[7] "The early universe / CERN. All matter in the universe was formed in one explosive event 13.7 billion years ago—the Big Bang." Accessed December 28, 2020, https://home.cern/science/physics/early-universe

same coin … *So energy and matter are really the same thing*"[8] (italics added). Completely interchangeable.

Mindful of what CERN and Professor Koberlein have stated, there's a widely believed misconception that scientists have been able to create and destroy elementary particles in laboratory experiments, which cannot be true because that would violate our previously mentioned law of the conservation of matter. Subsequently, the proper perception would be that scientists have never created or destroyed elementary particles, but rather have discovered how to make them appear and disappear back into their original form of energy—just as snowflakes are able to appear and disappear as well.

Moving on, that description would cause one to conclude that in the immediate big bang aftermath there were only two properties in existence—energy and elementary particles in all their forms—which simply isn't true because a third property also appeared. According to CERN,

> Just after the big bang, the Higgs Field was zero, but as the universe cooled and the temperature fell below a critical value, the field grew spontaneously so that any particle interacting with it acquired a mass. The more a particle interacts with this field, the heavier it is. Particles like the photon that do not interact with it are left with no mass at all. Like all fundamental fields, the Higgs field has an associated particle—the Higgs boson. The Higgs boson is the visible manifestation of the Higgs field, rather like a wave at the surface of the sea.[9]

[8] Brian Koberlein, "How Are Energy and Matter the Same?" Universe Today, November 26, 2014, https://www.universetoday.com/116615/how-are-energy-and-matter-the-same/#:~:text=So%20energy%20and%20matter%20are,are%20related%20through%20general%20relativity.&text=So%20in%20a%20way%2C%20energy,aspects%20of%20the%20same%20thing.

[9] CERN, "The Brout-Englert-Higgs Mechanism," accessed December 28, 2020, https://home.cern/science/physics/higgs-boson.

Just as elementary particles first began to appear as energy cooled, so too did the Higgs Field, which I theorize contains the light of our laws of knowledge simply because all energy and all elementary particles flow through the Higgs Field and are forced to interact with it in accordance with its "will."

Enter the superforce.

American Physicist Alan Guth used the term *superforce* to describe how the big bang expansion of our universe began:

> The universe expanded even faster than light. Faster than the cosmic speed limit, the ultimate speed according to Einstein ... Guth called his theory Inflation. In the earliest moments of creation, for instance, scientists believe that the four known forces of nature, including gravity and electromagnetism, were actually combined into a single Superforce.
>
> During the Big Bang, this Superforce split into the four known forces, but before it split, when the universe was incredibly small, Einstein's laws of physics, including the one that says nothing moves faster than light, didn't apply yet.
>
> Maybe at that moment something happened that caused the universe to expand even faster than light. So fast that it locked in the uniformity it had when the universe was still small.[10]

Compare that with Professor Paul Davies's statement, quoted earlier:

---

[10] The History Channel, "*The Universe*, S1E14 'Beyond the Big Bang,'" March 8, 2017, YouTube video, 1:13:55, https://www.youtube.com/watch?v=OkwO8Kq8RIU

> Together these investigations point towards a
> compelling idea, that all nature is ultimately
> controlled by the activities of a single *superforce*. The
> superforce would have the power to bring the universe
> into being and to furnish it with light, energy, matter,
> and structure. But the superforce would amount to
> more than just a creative agency. It would represent
> and amalgamation of matter, spacetime, and force
> into an integrated and harmonious framework that
> bestows upon the universe a hitherto unsuspected
> unity.[11]

Notice, both Professors Guth and Davies theorized that a superforce initiated the big bang's expansion of our universe, which means that our superforce of energy was the only thing in the universe that ever manifested out of nothing, while elementary particles and the Higgs Field (laws of knowledge) both appeared from it, much the way snowflakes appear, as its released energy began to cool.

As I will expound upon, since the superforce exists in a three-in-one state of singularity, as do the "tangible" bodies of the Trinity, then the superforce exists as eternal, with no beginning or end. It has never "manifested out of nothing" simply because it is the eternal physical being of God, thus making the four known fundamental forces of nature, and God, both omnipotent.

Regardless, because the superforce was comprised of the four known forces of nature, and because elementary particles and the Higgs Field both appeared from their original form of energy as it cooled, then that means the superforce actually contained within itself the totality of our universe, being:

---

[11] Davies, *Superforce*, 5–6.

1. The four known fundamental forces of nature: [12]

   A. The strong force (it holds the atomic nucleus together)
   B. The electromagnetic force (it causes interactions between charges)
   C. The weak force (it causes beta decay)
   D. The gravitational force (it causes interaction between states with energy). Gravity is space and time.[13]

2. Elementary particles that exist as three families of matter, with each family having different forms:[14]

   A. Quarks
   B. Leptons
   C. Bosons

3. Ever-expanding space filled with the light of our laws of knowledge, in the form of the Higgs Field and the Higgs boson. Therefore, as the universe expands into the infinite void of nothingness, as Paul Davies had described, then it's the space of the Higgs Field that fills that void of nothingness with the light of our laws of knowledge.

   Mindful of that, "Fundamental physics has always led the way in unifying knowledge."[15] Also, "perhaps the greatest scientific discovery of all time is that nature is written in mathematical code. We do not know the reason for this."[16]

---

[12] Particle Classification, accessed December 28, 2020, http://electron6.phys.utk.edu/phys250/modules/module%206/particle_classification.htm
[13] Davies, *Superforce*, 142.
[14] http://electron6.phys.utk.edu/phys250/modules/module%206/particle_classification.htm
[15] Davies, *Superforce*, 102.
[16] Davies, *Superforce*, 51.

In addition, understand, "A law would be useless if it were so restrictive that it permitted only one possible pattern of behavior. It would then become a description of the world rather than a true law."[17]

Finally, "A professional scientist is so immersed in unraveling the laws of nature that he forgets how remarkable it is that there are these laws in the first place. Because science presupposes rational laws, the scientist rarely stops to thing about why these laws exist."[18]

In conjunction with that, traditional Christian theology describes the Trinity as having three attributes:

1. Omniscience, while nothing is more all-knowing than the light of the laws of knowledge.
2. Omnipresence, while nothing is more all-present than elementary particles in all their forms.
3. Omnipotence, while nothing is more all-powerful than the four known fundamental forces of nature.

Next, know that the word *Trinity* does not occur in the Bible. Traditional Christianity used the word *Trinity* to, more or less, figuratively describe the Godhead's character, while the Bible uses the word *matrix* to, more or less, figuratively describe the Godhead's physical being. Science, on the other hand, uses the word *space-time* to, more or less, explain the general workings of the universe.

Expounding that even further, we cannot see the Father, Son, or Holy Spirit any more than we can see the four fundamental forces of nature, elementary particles, or the Higgs Field as our laws of knowledge, because each exists as a form of the exact

---

[17] Davies, *Superforce*, 53.
[18] Davies, *Superforce*, 223.

same thing, which simultaneously exists in three separate and distinct forms.

Therefore, with Trinity being the intangible character of God, and the matrix of our subatomic realm as His three-part tangible being, we've been deceived by the cloak of terminology. Hence:

- What science calls the subatomic realm, the Bible calls the matrix.
- What science calls elementary particles in all their forms, the Bible calls the Son.
- What science calls energy fields, such as the Higgs Field, the Bible calls the Father.
- What science calls the four known fundamental forces of nature, the Bible calls the Holy Spirit.
- What science calls the creation of the universe, the Bible calls the first couple of days.

Bringing this full circle, the totality of our universe is literally nothing more than the by-products of the Trinity's self-interaction, which began at Its point of singularity known as the big bang.

The reason we haven't been able to perceive the Lord's omnipresent nature is because He physically exists as our three invisible subatomic building blocks of all things, being invisible, intangible, and hidden from us in plain sight; or, as Hebrews 11:3 reads, "things which are seen were not made of things which do appear."

This means that the things we see in this world were not made from what we actually see, but rather from the invisible, intangible, subatomic properties that we cannot see—the invisible, intangible Trinity in infinite forms of continuous self-interaction, as this comparison chart helps explain:

H$_2$O exists as:	The Trinity as:	Conjunction	The matrix of our subatomic realm exists as:
Gas (Vapor)	The Father	Omniscience	The Higgs Field, and the Higgs boson, which I theorize exists as the light of the laws of knowledge in all its forms.
Solid (Ice)	The Son	Omnipresence	Elementary particles in all their forms.
Liquid (Water)	The Holy Spirit	Omnipotence	The four known forces of nature.

This means that every scholarly field literally studies the Trinity in a different form:

1. Quantum Physics studies the Trinity on a subatomic level.
2. Astronomy studies the Trinity on a macro level.
3. Chemistry studies the Trinity on the molecular level.
4. Psychology studies how we choose to interact with the Trinity and each other.
5. Christianity studies how the Lord desires for humankind to interact with the character of the Trinity, as well as with each other.
6. The medical profession studies the Trinity in human bodily form.
7. Entomology studies the Trinity in insect form.
8. And so on down the line.

Thus, these are not separate subjects of study but rather the same singular subject (God) as studied from different points-of-view. Along with that, physicists know things about the Trinity that astronomers do not, who know things about the Trinity that carpenters do not, who know things about the Trinity that steel workers do not, etc.

This means that every single person who ever lived has unknowingly interacted with the Trinity in every facet of his or her life, as everything we see, smell, taste, and touch is literally nothing more than the Trinity in ever-changing forms, all of which began at the Trinity's big bang point of singularity.

Mindful of that, humankind has long struggled with an age-old question: Can God make a stone so heavy that He cannot lift it?

This conflicting question is really a paradox, which is answered by a type of zero-sum game. God physically exists as the subatomic properties from which that stone was created, as well as the fundamental forces required to move it; therefore, to move that stone, the Trinity merely interacts with Itself.

Which would lead us to ask, If this is true, then why does the Bible read with the Father, Son, and Holy Spirit having different characteristics/personalities?

Consider that ice, water, and vapor, even though singular as H_2O, each have different forms and characteristics, being their personalities, so to speak.

The laws of knowledge, elementary particles, and the four fundamental forces of nature, even though singular as a superforce, each have different forms and characteristics, being their personalities, so to speak.

The Father, Son, and Holy Spirit, even though singular as God, each have different forms and characteristics, being their personalities, so to speak, as:

- The Higgs Field somehow has the character of the Father, laws of knowledge, attached to it.

- Elementary particles in all their forms somehow have the character of the Son attached to them.

- The four fundamental forces of nature somehow have the character of the Holy Spirit attached to them.

With that in mind, consider this comparison chart in order to better understand how man was made in the image of God:

Man's three bodies and voices:	God's three bodies and voices:
A soul (which contains your will, intellect, and emotions to make you different from everyone else), with a voice called "reasoning."	The Higgs Field, as the light of the laws of knowledge, with a voice called "God the Father."
A physical body, with a voice called "our five-senses."	Elementary particles in all their forms, with a voice called "the Son."
A spirit (being your lifeforce), with a voice called "conscience," being your internal sense of right and wrong.	The four known forces of nature, with a voice called "the Holy Spirit."

Therefore, we're blessed to interact with the Trinity because of the mysterious manner in which their three different personalities are somehow attached to their three "bodies," commonly referred to as *persons*.

Which leads us to Exodus 3:14, when the Lord told Moses His name was "I AM THAT I AM."

This is really more of a description then a name, but a description of what?

I Am the Trinity, being the intangible three-in-one character of God.

I Am the matrix, being the more tangible three-in-one bodies of God.

This illuminates Revelation 1:8: "I am Alpha and Omega, the beginning and the ending, saith the Lord, which is, and which was, and which is to come, the Almighty."

Notice, the Lord described Himself in two ways, the first being:

Alpha: The beginning moment of His superforce of singularity, being the smallest of the small.

Omega: The ending totality of our universe as a whole, being the biggest of the big.

As well as space that contains everything in between.

With the second description being:

"Which is, and which was, and which is to come, the Almighty," meaning past, present, and future, simultaneously.

Amazingly, that two-part self-description perfectly defines what science calls space-time.

Hence:

- The Bible speaks of the matrix but never defines it.
- Christianity speaks of the Trinity, though the Bible never mentions it.
- Science speaks of space-time.

All of these are, once again, the exact same thing, only clothed in different terminology.

Next, we should understand that the only thing in existence during our pre–big bang state was the singular Trinity in the form of that subatomic superforce egg, surrounded by nothing, as Professor Paul Davies stated:

> Therefore the universe does not expand *into* anything,
> it simply grows in scale everywhere … there is no
> space outside the universe. Rather, it is more accurate

> to envisage the big bang as an event in which space itself came into being … Space came out of the big bang, and not the other way around. The big bang, then, was not an event which occurred within the universe; it was the coming-into-being of the universe, it its entirety, from literally nothing.[19]

Which simply means that in the beginning of time the only thing in existence was the Trinity in Its superforce form, surrounded by nothing, which the Trinity's self-interaction continuously expands into. Therefore, as previously mentioned, space in form of the Higgs Field simply replaces that expanse of nothingness with knowledge.

With that said, this next point should be obvious. Because everything exists as the Trinity in ever-changing forms, then in the mind of God humankind has no rights, only privileges. That's what Lucifer didn't understand when he and the others rebelled—that everything was God and therefore they had no right to demand anything—as all they possessed was the nature of their characters and the privileges which the Trinity had bestowed upon them.

With the mystery of the Lord's omnipresent nature now solved, it should be easier to understand how you are in Him, and He is in you, and how He is easily able to simultaneously hear the prayers of all humankind.

The Lord is sovereign, as the entire universe exists as Him in ever-changing forms.

In turn, this revelation births some marvelous insights into numerous scripture passages as well. First, "I will never leave thee, nor forsake thee" (Hebrews 13:5).

---

[19] Davies, *Superforce*, 15–16.

He can't because He physically exists as the building blocks of all things. This includes our own physical bodies, which exist as the Trinity in another form.

Meaning our souls are contained within Him, thus revealing that the nature of our character is the only thing that we truly possess. We then reveal the nature of our character to others through our words, deeds, and actions, as well as reflecting back to ourselves through the mirror of how we handle our tests and trials in life.

Likewise, Satan's soul is contained within a spiritual body that is literally nothing more than the Trinity in a different form as well, through which Satan's character is trapped within the Trinity and can never escape, forever powerless to defeat the Lord.

This means that all nonbelievers, and even criminals who've evaded capture, are guaranteed justice because their souls are also contained within physical bodies that exist as the Trinity in different forms. Therefore, just like anyone else, they can only escape hell by sincerely accepting Jesus Christ as their Lord and Savior.

Thus all of life is revealed to be a fixed game that the Trinity can never lose, as the totality of the universe is nothing more than the Trinity in ever-changing forms of self-interaction.

Deeper still, every saint in heaven will experience the blessings of the Trinity in Their ever-changing forms of heaven, while every sinner in hell will experience the curses of the Trinity in Their ever-changing forms of hell. Heaven and hell are each made from the exact same subatomic building blocks of properties as we are, minus the mass.

Or, as David stated in Psalm 139:8, "If I ascend up into heaven, thou art there: if I make my bed in hell, behold, thou art there."

Next, Matthew 3:9 reads, "God is able of these stones to raise up children unto Abraham."

God is able to raise children from those stones because they're made from the same building blocks of subatomic properties as is the human body, as those molecules simply need to change from stone to human bodily form.

> The thing that hath been, it is that which shall be; and that which is done is that which shall be done: and there is no new thing under the sun. (Ecclesiastes 1:9)

There is nothing new under the sun because everything began from the big bang's point of singularity, making everything exist as the exact same thing in a different form.

> Through faith we understand that the worlds were framed by the word of God, so that things which are seen were not made of things which do appear. (Hebrews 11:3)

Contrary to many Pentecostal preachers, God the Father does not speak things into existence in accordance with His faith, per se; rather, energy and subatomic particles always interact to form whatever the laws of knowledge (Father) desires.

Hence:

- "All things were made by him [Jesus]; and without him was not any thing made that was made" (John 1:3).
  All things are made from elementary particles (the Son), and without them nothing is made that is made.

- "I [Jesus] said, I go unto the Father: for my Father is greater than I" (John 14:28).
  Just as God the Father is greater than Jesus, so too are the laws of knowledge greater than elementary particles, as particles (Son) always obey the laws of knowledge (Father).

- "Ye shall receive power, after that the Holy Ghost is come upon you" (Acts 1:8).
  The Holy Ghost physically exists as the four known forces of nature, which is power, as energy (Spirit) also obeys the laws of knowledge (Father).

With regard to the Trinity being one:

- "I and my Father are one" (John 10:30).
- "He that hath seen me hath seen the Father" (John 14:9).
- "Hear, O Israel: The Lord our God is one Lord" (Deuteronomy 6:4).
- "In him dwelleth all the fulness of the Godhead bodily" (Colossians 2:9).

Next, let's consider other verses in which humankind interacts with the Trinity:

O taste and see that the Lord is good. (Psalm 34:8)

Everything you taste, as well as see, hear, and touch, is literally the Trinity in ever-changing forms.

Then spake Joshua to the Lord … and he said in the sight of Israel, Sun, stand thou still upon Gibeon; and thou, Moon, in the valley of Ajalon. And the sun stood still, and the moon stayed. (Joshua 10:12–13)

With the Trinity physically existing as our subatomic realm, then it would be quite simple for Him to control the sun and the moon.

Whatever is not of faith is sin. (Romans 14:23)

Using this newfound revelation of the Trinity's physical being, we could redefine sin as any form of interaction with the Trinity that runs contrary to the will of the Trinity.

In turn, this helps us better understand what the tree of life and the tree of the knowledge of good and evil in the garden of Eden symbolize:

- Obedience: To partake from the tree of life is to interact with the Trinity in accordance with the will of the Trinity, through which types of blessings will ensue. For instance, Abel obediently interacted with the Trinity when he gave an offering that was in accordance with the will of the Trinity, through which types of blessings ensued.

- Disobedience: To partake from the tree of the knowledge of good and evil is to interact with the Trinity contrary to the will of the Trinity, through which types of curses will ensue. For instance, Cain disobediently interacted with the Trinity when he gave an offering that was contrary to the will of the Trinity, through which types of curses ensued.

(Please know that the day six chapter goes into much greater detail on those two trees.)

- God is a Spirit: and they that worship him must worship him in spirit and in truth. (John 4:24)

What is a spirit? Oftentimes we consider a spirit to be a living, intangible entity that, for whatever reason, we're still able to interact with. The Bible has numerous examples of angelic beings that appeared in order to give messages to both men and women.

Following that line of reasoning, consider that knowledge, thoughts, dreams, visions, and emotions are all intangible properties that we're also able to interact with, as they are forms of spiritual interaction.

Therefore, since God the Father and the light of the laws of knowledge are both intangible yet allow us to interact with them, then it only stands to reason that they are also the very same thing. This in turn reveals in a greater way how growing in knowledge allows us to live more of the life of God—as growing in knowledge is literally growing in God the Father.

Next, Genesis 1:1 reads, "In the beginning God created the heaven and the earth." Since God's three-in-one singularity was our big bang superforce, consider these questions in regard to Genesis 1:1:

- What if the word *God* is figurative for our big bang superforce?
- What if the word *heaven* is figurative for our intangible subatomic realm?
- What if the word *earth* is figurative for the tangible substances that the earth would later be made from?

With that in mind, try reading Genesis 1:1–3, slightly reworded:

> *In the beginning God,* as the superforce big bang,
> *created the heaven,* our intangible subatomic realm,
> *and the earth,* our initial tangible substances that the earth would
>   later be accumulated from,
> *And the earth was without form, and void; and darkness was upon the*
>   *face of the deep*—without form and void because the earth
>   hadn't been created yet, as darkness still covered the area
>   where the earth would one day be.
> *And the Spirit of God,* being the recently released fundamental
>   forces of nature,
> *moved upon the face of the waters,* newly formed subatomic particles
>   in all their forms that appeared when the universe cooled.
> *And God,* as the light of the laws of knowledge,
> *said, Let there be light: and there was,* eventually but not immediately,
>   light.

Now that makes sense, and also reveals the big bang theory to be a biblical principle first recorded by Moses some 3,500 years ago.

This now raises the question, How old is the universe?

Understand that the totality of our current technological advancements, formulas, and theories are so precise that science can now prove many facets of space-time, or give extremely accurate approximations, such as the age of the universe. To explain this, Maria Temming wrote,

> The age of the universe is approximately 13.77 billion years. This age is calculated by measuring the distances and radial velocities of other galaxies, most of which are flying away from our own at speeds proportional to their distances. Using the current expansion rate of the universe, we can imagine "rewinding" the universe to the point where everything was contained in a singularity, and calculate how much time must have passed between that moment (the Big Bang) and the present.[20]

Unfortunately, we're not finished yet, because this theory now presents us with at least two paradoxes that must be resolved.

First, Acts 17:29 reads, "Forasmuch then as we are the offspring of God, we ought not to think that the Godhead is like unto gold, or silver, or stone, graven by art and man's device."

If the universe does exist as the Trinity in ever-changing forms, then how do we reconcile that the Godhead is *not* "like unto gold, silver, or stone, graven by art and man's device"?

It's perception.

---

[20] Maria Temming, "What Is the Age of the Universe?" *Sky and Telescope*, July 18, 2014, https://skyandtelescope.org/astronomy-resources/age-of-the-universe/.

The Lord doesn't want to be worshipped for what He is, meaning the tangible by-products created from His self-interaction, but rather for who He is, meaning the intangible nature of His character.

The second paradox is found in the nature of His omnipresent form.

Many preachers love to proclaim that God is omnipresent, only to later state that He doesn't exist within sinners but only in born-again Christians.

That's a blatant contradiction.

If the Lord doesn't exist within sinners, then that means there are places in the universe where He does not exist; hence, by nature, He'd cease to be omnipresent.

You can't have it both ways. Either He's omnipresent or He isn't.

This paradox is also reconciled through the sound reasoning of our perceptions; in fact, Exodus chapter 3, when the Lord revealed himself to Moses in the form of a burning bush, provides us with our very best example of understanding.

Obviously, the Lord was in the burning bush, which is also a misnomer.

Don't forget that the Lord is omnipresent, which provides us with our first insights of reconciliation.

While in the burning bush, the Lord was also with the Eskimos in Alaska, the forebears of the Incas in South America, and everywhere else in the world simultaneously—with one exception: for whatever reason, the Lord chose not to reveal Himself to them.

The Lord had chosen to reveal Himself only to Moses, and only at that specific time and place.

Along with that, every single moment of Moses's life, the Lord was with Moses just as much as He was with him at the burning bush— with one exception: for whatever reason, the Lord chose not to reveal Himself to Moses during those times.

It's that revelation of how and when the Lord had chosen to reveal Himself to Moses, and no one else, that reconciles our paradox of how the omnipresent nature of the Lord must also exist within sinners.

However, let me first ask, What's the one thing that every living creature, regardless of species, has in common?

It's the breath of life, as the breath of life is what separates living creatures from inanimate objects.

You see, inanimate objects, as well as our physical bodies, are all one with the universe because they're all comprised of the exact same subatomic building blocks of creation; however, the soul of a living creature is somehow separate from the universe.

Know that your soul is comprised of your will, intellect, and emotions and makes you different from everyone else, though no one knows just what exactly a soul is made from. Odds are that living souls exist as some type of computer code that allows us to interact with the matrix but with free will.

Therefore, as we grow in knowledge, various types of data are inputted to us, which in turn helps us better interact with the world around us.

Regardless, the Holy Spirit is our breath of life, while all living creatures from dust mites to blue whales have the exact same breath of life within them, meaning that saints and sinners alike also have the exact same breath of life, being the exact same amount of the Holy Spirit.

With just one difference:

The Holy Spirit hasn't revealed His indwelling presence to them, but only to born-again Christians who have sincerely received Jesus Christ as their personal Lord and Savior, as their born-again experience was the moment in which the Holy Spirit "turned their light on."

Think of His revealed presence in these terms:

Unbeknownst to the apostle Paul, the Holy Spirit was just as much in him when he was Saul as He was in Paul after his born-again experience. It's just that the Holy Spirit didn't reveal His indwelling presence to him until *after* he accepted Christ, which was when the Holy Spirit "turned Paul's light on."

Paul's born-again experience was to him as the burning bush was to Moses—and no one else.

Once again, if the Holy Spirit didn't exist within Saul while Saul was still a sinner, then that means there was someplace in the universe where the Holy Spirit did not exist; therefore, by nature, He'd cease to be omnipresent.

Once again, you can't have it both way. Either the Lord is omnipresent or He isn't, which then becomes a type of paradox that must become resolved through sound reasoning.

Similarly, with the Trinity physically existing as our building blocks of subatomic properties, then that means all knowledge, power, and authority exist both within and around us, while we've only been granted limited access to them. Some have more knowledge than others because they've actively sought to grow in the accumulated graces of knowledge, while prodigies have been, for whatever reason, granted greater access to knowledge.

This leads to a hard question: Following that line of reasoning, the Holy Spirit must have existed as Hitler's breath of life as well, so why didn't the Holy Spirit stop him?

The most obvious response would be, "What difference does it make if the Holy Spirit existed within Hitler or not? Either way the Holy Spirit had the power to stop him but chose not to."

A second response would be, "We know that the Holy Spirit exists within born-again Christians, many of whom have fallen from grace through personal sin, so why didn't the indwelling presence of the Holy Spirit stop them from sinning as well?"

Perhaps the Holy Spirit spoke warnings into each of their thought lives, warnings which their personal will chose to ignore.

Hence we arrive at this: the Holy Spirit must exist within evil men such as Hitler in order to give them their breath of life, only they never received the revelation of His indwelling presence within them, having never had their "light turned on."

Expounding further, it's commonly taught that Jesus and the apostle Paul had more of the Holy Spirit then others did or do. Both of these misnomers must also be reconciled through sound-reasoning.

Once again, every creature that's ever lived has had the exact same measure of the Holy Spirit within them, in the form of their breath of life—but with one exception, the depths to which the Holy Spirit has chosen to reveal Himself to them.

Ergo, it's not that Jesus or the apostle Paul had more of the Holy Spirit than anyone else, but rather the Holy Spirit had revealed Himself to them in greater ways, which in turned empowered their spiritual lights to shine exponentially brighter than the others.

This means that Jesus's and Paul's greatly increased levels of revelation knowledge had empowered them with greater levels of the life of God, which then manifested itself to the world around them through the nature of their words, deeds, and actions.

Not only that, but the Lord then magnified their light by confirming the words that they spoke with signs following, in the form of the gifts of the Spirit (Mark 16:20).

This means that the born-again experience is like a dimmer switch, as our greater levels of obedience will result in greater levels of revelation knowledge, which in turn empowers us with greater levels of the life of God, which then continuously brightens our spiritual light through the nature of our words, deeds, and actions. Unrepented sin eventually "turns our light off."

Finally, with this chapter fresh in mind, let's read Genesis 1:2–5 slightly reworded:

> *And the Spirit of God* (as the four fundamental forces of nature) *moved upon the face of the waters* (The Son as elementary particles in all His forms).
> *And God* (The Father as the light of the laws of knowledge) *said, Let there be light: and there was* (progressively but not immediately) *light.*
> *And God saw the light, that it was good: and God divided the light from the darkness.*
> *And God called the light Day, and the darkness he called Night. And the evening and the morning were the first day.*

Now that makes sense.

The Matrix

God is a circle whose center is everywhere and circumference nowhere.

—Voltaire

Theologians commonly define the word *matrix* as a womb, but that definition is only partly true because a womb is literally nothing more than energy, elementary particles, and knowledge, all comprised together in a different form. Thus making a womb but one small piece to our infinitely larger universe's three-in-one state-of-singularity puzzle.

To better understand this, let's consider some examples:

Picture standing next to a campfire. Sense its heat, and notice the ashes that collect underneath the fire, not to mention the smoke that drifts away.

Next, imagine a casket-less corpse buried underground as worms and other insects digest its matter and then convert and excrete that matter into other forms. Trees and plants also feed upon its decay, which in turn produces new wood and oxygen to be released back into the atmosphere.

Finally, watch an acorn form into a seedling and then slowly grow to maturity.

From our point of view, we perceive such phenomena as types of creation and destruction because of the manner in which they affect our ability to use them; however, from the Lord's point of view, nothing is ever created or destroyed but merely changes form.

In essence, that's the workings of the matrix, being our subatomic realm in which nothing is ever created or destroyed, but merely changes form; after all:

- The molecules in the burning wood weren't destroyed but rather changed form into such things as smoke and ashes.
- When that person died, his or her body was converted into an inanimate object, the molecules of which eventually changed form, into many other forms as well.
- Finally, that acorn was able to grow to maturity because of the manner in which molecules from other sources had changed form in order to fuel that acorn's growth.

The Bible has numerous verses that mention the matrix but never explains what the matrix actually is (italics here are added):

> That thou shalt set apart unto the Lord all that openeth *the matrix*, and every firstling that cometh of a beast which thou hast; the males shall be the Lord's. (Exodus 13:12)

> And it come to pass, when Pharaoh would hardly let us go, that the Lord slew all firstborn in the land of Egypt, both the firstborn of man, and the firstborn of beast; therefore I sacrifice to the Lord all that openeth *the matrix*, being males; but all the firstborn of my children I redeem. (Exodus 13:15)

> All that openeth *the matrix* is mine; and every firstling among thy cattle, whether ox or sheep, that is male. (Exodus 34:19)

> And I, behold, I have taken the Levites from among
> the children of Israel instead of all the firstborn that
> openeth *the matrix* among the children of Israel:
> therefore the Levites shall be mine. (Numbers 3:12)

> Every thing that openeth *the matrix* in all flesh, which
> they bring unto the Lord, whether it be of men or
> beasts, shall be thing: nevertheless, the firstborn of
> man shalt thou surely redeem, and the firstling of
> unclean beasts shalt thou redeem. (Numbers 18:15)

You might have noticed that each of those verses describes various types of birth, as a womb is commonly used to describe the matrix; however, once again, a womb is literally nothing more than energy, elementary particles, and knowledge in a different form.

As everything in the universe, with the exception of living souls, is literally nothing more than infinite forms of inanimate objects, which all exist as the exact same thing in a different form. However, it's only in the womb that a living soul is imparted into some type of a living creature, regardless of the species, which in turn empowers that creature to interact with the Trinity in all Its inanimate forms. After all, a corpse reveals that the physical body of any life form is nothing more than another type of inanimate object.

Accordingly, the birth of a living soul is the opening of the matrix, being when that living soul is first consciously able to interact with the Trinity in all Its inanimate forms of continuous self-interaction.

With these things in mind, consider what the Lord said to Moses in Exodus 33:20–23 (italics added):

> Thou canst not see my face: for there shall no man
> see me, and live. And the Lord said, Behold, there is
> a place by me, and thou shalt stand upon a rock: And

it shall come to pass, while my glory passeth by, that I
will put thee in a cleft of the rock, and will cover thee
with my hand while I pass by: And I will take away
mine hand, and thou shalt see *my back parts*: but my
face shall not be seen.

Traditional Christian theology believes that the Lord has a literal
physical body, which Moses was allowed to see the back of. Others
more carefully interpret *back parts* to figuratively mean history: that
God Almighty placed Moses in the cleft of the rock in order to show
Moses His history.

What's His history? It's twofold.

On a macroscale His history exists as the tangible properties formed
during the six-day Genesis account of creation, which Moses received
while in the cleft of the rock.

On a microscale it's the matrix, being our subatomic realm of three-
in-one intangible substances.

Or, in other words, "so that things which are seen were not made of
things which do appear" (Hebrews 11:3).

Our tangible natural world that we can see is made from an intangible
spiritual world that we cannot be see, thus existing as a paradox of
the exact same thing in a different form.

With that in mind, we've already examined the first day of God's
history in which He created our invisible, intangible subatomic
realm. The creation on day two, however, is quite different because
that's when He began to create our visible, tangible universe.

However, before He was able to create our tangible universe, He
had to first create the substance of mass whereby to empower His
intangible properties to be converted into tangibleness.

Crossing a Bridge
Called Mass

Perhaps the greatest scientific discovery of all time is that nature is written in mathematical code. We do not know the reason for this, but it is the single most important fact that enables us to understand, control, and predict the outcome of physical processes.

—Paul Davies

Angels and demons are all around us yet are invisible, intangible, and hidden from us in plain sight, which leads many to wonder what their spiritual bodies are made from.

Simple common sense reveals that they're made from the exact same intangible subatomic properties that we are made from, minus the mass, as their lack of mass is what empowers them to be hidden from us in plain sight.

Yet where does our mass come from?

As far as we know, there are two sources for the vast majority of our universe's mass:

1. The Higgs Field, which plays a minor role of about 2 percent.
2. The kinetic and potential energy that exists within atoms, which plays a major role of about 98 percent.

First, regarding the Higgs Field, Arvin Ash states,

> It's theorized that different particles interact differently
> with the field. The particles that interact with it more
> intensely have greater mass than particles that don't
> interact with it as much.
>
> Let's use the analogy of water.
>
> Certain shapes, like a pointed nose fish, would be
> able to flow very quickly through the water because
> of its low resistance, while a block would have higher
> resistance, and would interact with it to a greater
> degree. Subatomic particles interact with the Higgs
> Field in a similar way.[21]

Notice, the Higgs Field has been likened to water; hence, "the Spirit of
God moved upon the face of the waters," meaning this description of
the Higgs Field could be included with our Genesis 1:2 interpretation
of waters.

Along with that, remember that liquid, solid, and gas exist as the
three states of matter, whereby we can liken matter, H_2O, and the
Trinity as:

Matter	H_2O	The Trinity
Liquid	Water	The Father as the light of the laws of knowledge, a.k.a. the Higgs Field.
Solid	Ice	The Son as elementary particles in all their forms.
Gas	Vapor	The Holy Spirit as the four fundamental forces of nature (energy).

Second, regarding the kinetic and potential energy found in atoms,
Arvin Ash also points out,

---

[21] Arvin Ash, "The Higgs Boson and Higgs Field Explained with Simple Analogy," September
15, 2018, YouTube video, 2:53, https://www.youtube.com/watch?v=zAazvVIGK-c.

Your mass equals all the mass of the atoms in your body, while gravity acting on that mass gives you your weight ….

But where does the mass of the atom come from? […]

Only about 2% of the mass of the universe is directly due to the Higgs Field. So where does the other 98% come from? …

It comes from the kinetic and potential energy spinning within the proton ….

Remember that $e = mc^2$

Which can be converted to $m = \frac{e}{c^2}$ […]

The mass comes from the kinetic and potential energy of these quarks whizzing around each other at high speed, so that the vast majority of the mass of particles, at the fundamental level, is nothing but energy swarming around inside the nucleus of atoms, that manifest itself as mass.[22]

Sometime after the big bang, the Trinity's self-interaction empowered the intangible properties of our subatomic realm to develop atoms, and within those atoms existed then the kinetic and potential energy needed to create the substance of mass, which in turn is what creates tangible properties.

---

[22] Arvin Ash, "The Shocking Source of All Mass—It's Not What You Think. Where Does Mass Come From?" September 21, 2018, YouTube video, 00:35, https://www.youtube.com/watch?v=2kUFs6_DBrM.

DAY TWO

The Tangible Universe

Good ideas are always crazy until they're not.

—Larry Page

According to Professor Paul Davies, "The word universe has the same origin as *unity* and *one*. It means, literally, the totality of things considered as a whole. Curiously, the word *wholly* derives from the same origin as *holy*, which reflects the deep mystical and metaphysical associations of cosmology."[23]

With that in mind, Genesis 1:6–8 reads:

> And God said, Let there be a firmament in the midst of the waters, and let it divide the waters from the waters. And God made the firmament, and divided the waters which were under the firmament from the waters which were above the firmament: and it was

---

[23] Davies, *Superforce*, 206.

so. And God called the firmament Heaven. And the evening and the morning were the second day.

These waters can't literally be our H_2O waters of today because those waters weren't created until day three. So what could *waters* here figuratively represent?

They're our invisible, intangible, darkened seas of subatomic properties (energy, elementary particles, and the light of the laws of knowledge) were caused to appear on day one. However, the firmament of heaven probably existed as our earliest formation of mineral dust, the earliest form of tangible mass, which progressively stuck together in order to eventually accumulate into meteors, planets, and stars, which humankind has long called *the heavens*.

According to planetary scientist William Hartman:

> The theory that emerged was that the sun was surrounded by a cloud of dust and gas, and as that cloud cooled little grains of minerals formed. So all these little grains of minerals floating in this gaseous cloud are moving around the sun and they start to bump into each other.

In the zero gravity of space an experiment was conducted aboard the International Space Station in which grains of salt were placed in a plastic bag filled with water. When the bag was shaken,

> The particles immediately began to stick to each other by forming little clumps all held together by tiny static electric charges. Scientists realized that if grains of salt stuck together in space the so could the mineral grains in a solar dust cloud .... As mineral grains in the solar dust cloud bumped into each other, and

stuck together, they grew into small pieces of rock orbiting the sun. Over the next few million years some of them collided and grew bigger.[24]

Meaning mineral dust existed as the earliest stage of development from which our meteors and planets eventually accumulated.

Along with that, we consider heaven to be a place of great light, while we currently have only one great light that we know of, being the totality of our universe. The Planck Map[25] shows our universe as a whole, which also exists as a great light that divides the darkness of infinite "waters" that surround it.

Please keep in mind that the word *firmament* implies something tangible due to its density, while the word *waters* implies something less tangible, perhaps even figuratively intangible, due to its lesser density. Thus the firmament that separated the waters from the waters existed in different scales of development. For instance:

On a nanoscale: Atoms have mass, meaning they separate the darkened waters of elementary particles that surround them.

On a microscale: Early mineral dust had mass, meaning that mineral dust separated the darkened waters from the darkened waters that surround them.

On a macroscale: Such things as meteors, stars, and planets have mass, meaning they separate the darkened waters from the darkened waters that surround them.

---

[24] The History Channel, "*The Universe*, S1E14 'Beyond the Big Bang.'" September 4, 2007, YouTube video, 3:00, https://www.youtube.com/watch?v=nhgyorQQXtU&t=338s.

[25] Jennifer Welsh, "Five Things We Didn't Know About the Universe before This New Map," *Business Insider*, March 21, 2013, https://www.businessinsider.com/plank-map-of-the-universe-2013-3.

Regardless, because the biblical six days of creation chronologically unfold in direct correlation with science's current levels of accumulated knowledge, then the firmament's most likely interpretation exists as our earliest forms of mineral dust which had been formed in the gaseous clouds of our cosmos.

DAY THREE

The Creation of Earth

If you truly love nature, you will find beauty everywhere.

—Vincent Van Gogh

And God said, Let the waters under heaven be gathered together unto one place, and let the dry land appear: and it was so. And God called the dry land earth; and the gathering together of the waters called the Seas: and God saw that it was good. And God said, Let the earth bring forth grass, the herb yielding seed, and the fruit tree yielding fruit after his kind. Whose seed is in itself, upon the earth: and it was so. And the earth brought forth grass, and herb yielding seed after his kind, and the tree yielding fruit, whose seed was in itself, after his kind: and God saw that it was good. And the evening and the morning were the third day. (Genesis 1:9–13)

Of all the days of creation day three is the most literally written, though heaven in this passage refers to the earth's atmosphere, which we also call "the heavens."

Where did all of the earth's water come from?

The History Channel has a program called, *How the Earth Was Made*, with a specific episode entitled, "Birth of the Earth," which stated: "New evidence showing how our water arrived on Earth has emerged from a meteorite that fell in 1998, but has only recently been analyzed." As cosmic mineralogist Michael Zolensky stated, "This meteorite contains grains of table salt."

Each grain of salt contained a minute droplet of water, and that water arrived by meteorites which continuously pummeled the molten Earth over millions of years during its formation. Those countless meteorites then melted into our molten earth and caused it to grow, while at the same time depositing their salt and water droplets into the molten mix, and in turn eventually culminated into all of the salt and water that we now have today.[26]

Yet, how old is the earth? "In 1897 Physicist Ernest Rutherford figured out that measuring radioactive decay could accurately date the age of rocks."[27]

> In the early 1950s the American Geologist C. C. Patterson tried a new approach using meteorites. He knew that meteorites must have clumped together from the same mineral grains in space that formed the Earth, and that happened at the same time as the Earth was born.

---

[26] The History Channel, "*How the Earth Was Made*, S2E3, 'Birth of the Earth,'" December 8, 2009, YouTube video, 30:00, https://www.youtube.com/watch?v=vfovimAa16o&t=1680s.
[27] History Channel, *How the Earth Was Made*.

So, if he could date a meteorite he should get the true age of the Earth. […]

Patterson dated the samples and was amazed by the results. The meteorite was a staggering 4.5 billion years old. Meaning that the Earth was also born 4.5 billion years ago. Patterson had solved the problem that had defeated scientists for centuries.[28]

---

[28] History Channel, *How the Earth Was Made.*

The Creation of Angels

And I beheld, and I heard the voice of many angels round about the throne and the beasts and the elders: and the number of them was ten thousand times ten thousand, and thousands of thousands.

—Revelation 5:11

And God said, Let there be lights in the firmament of the heaven to divide the day from the night; and let them be for signs, and for seasons, and for days, and years: And let them be for lights in the firmament of the heaven to give light upon the earth: and it was so. *And God made two great lights; the greater light to rule the day, and the lesser light to rule the night*: he made the stars also. And God set them in the firmament of the heaven to give light upon the earth, And to rule over the day and over the night, and to divide the light from the darkness: and God saw that it was good.

And the evening and the morning were the fourth day. (Genesis 1:14–19, italics added)

As mentioned in the introduction, "the greater light to rule the day, and the lesser light to rule the night" that had been created on day four cannot be our literal sun and moon, as many interpret, because the earth's plant life created on day three would have lacked the heat and photosynthesis needed to sustain it. This raises the question, What do those two lights figuratively represent?

They're angels.

When Lucifer rebelled, he took a third of the angels to collectively become "the lesser light to rule the night," while the faithful angels, being greater in numbers, collectively became "the greater light to rule the day," as each set of angels radiates types of spiritual light to us who exist naturally on the earth.

For instance, in Matthew 4:1–11, Jesus was led by the Spirit into the wilderness to be tempted of the devil. This was when He experienced "the lesser light to rule [His] night." Conversely, when the holy angels later came and ministered to Him, Jesus then experienced "the greater light to rule [His] day."

Mindful of that, science has long theorized that we live in a multidimensional world with other realms of existence, while our spirit realm of the Trinity, angels, ghosts, and demons, that exists all around us while hidden in plain sight, is obviously one of those realms. In fact, what we call the supernatural is actually a realm composed of the exact same subatomic properties that our physical bodies are created from, minus the mass, which is what allows the supernatural to remain hidden from us in plain sight. Thus miracles are nothing more than the Trinity's self-interaction to suddenly change form in ways that run contrary to our perception of scientific laws, whereby supernatural healings are merely unexpected rearrangements of subatomic properties.

In conjunction with that, human beings are created as a conjoining of spiritual and physical bodies, meaning we simultaneously exist in both the natural and supernatural realms. After all, our physical bodies have mass, which is what empowers us to interact with the natural world around us for as long as we live. However, at the time of death, our intangible spiritual bodies are finally empowered to escape the mass of our tangible physical bodies, which in turn ushers us into heaven's eternal blessings or hell's eternal curses.

Second, because our spiritual bodies are invisible, intangible, and massless, just like the Trinity, angels, ghosts, and demons, then we're also empowered to unknowingly interact with them through invisible, intangible, and massless avenues. For instance, angelic forces impart knowledge to us through their spiritual wavelengths of thoughts, dreams, and visions, which we must learn to interpret.

This is important because the language of man is literal, while the language of the spirit is figurative/symbolic. It's our ability to interpret (not translate) that converts the figurative language of the spirit into our more literal understandings.

I refer to this form of spiritual communication as the color-wheel spectrum of sin, as angels and demons exist as types of princes who reign over us through spiritual principalities that are color-coded to correspond with our emotions. This in turn influences the nature of our words, deeds, and actions to display our levels of Christlikeness, or satanic likeness, to the world around us.

———— ❧ ————

The Evolution of Our Prehistoric Era

> It is not the strongest of the species that survives, nor the most intelligent that survives, it is the one that is most adaptable to change.
>
> —Charles Darwin

The theory of evolution was popularized in 1859, when Charles Darwin published his book, *On the Origin of Species by Means of Natural Selection, or The Preservation of Favoured Races in the Struggle for Life*, though many believed it to be threat to the faith through its contradiction of scripture.

What no one back then understood, nor seemingly does anyone today, is that the theory of evolution exists in a near-perfect word-for-word agreement with the Genesis day five account of creation.

But how?

"Charles Darwin was reluctant to publish his views on life's origin. His only speculations on the subject are known from a private letter to his friend and colleague Joseph Hooker, in which he speaks of a 'warm little pond' in which the first molecules of life could have formed."[29]

Many decades later, postdoctoral research associate Sean Jordan wrote, "In recent years, many scientists have shifted from favouring a 'primordial soup' in pools of water to hydrothermal vents deep in the ocean as the original source of life on Earth."[30]

Notice, Darwin believed that life on Earth began in a "warm little pond," while Jordan wrote that many scientists have shifted to hydrothermal vents deep in the ocean.

Let's now compare those assertions with Genesis 1:20–23:

> And God said, *let the waters bring forth abundantly* the moving creature that hath life, and fowl that may fly above the earth in the open firmament of heaven. And God created great whales, and *every living creature which moveth,* which *the waters brought forth abundantly* after their kind, and every winged fowl after his kind: and God saw that it was good. And God blessed them, saying, Be fruitful, and multiply, and fill the waters in the seas, and let fowl multiply in the earth. And the evening and the morning were the fifth day. (italics added)

Notice, just as evolutionists also theorize, "every living creature which moveth" including the "fowl that … fly above the earth," originally came from the waters.

---

[29] Lucas Brouwers, "Did Life Evolve in a 'Warm Little Pond'?" *Scientific American,* February 16, 2012, https://blogs.scientificamerican.com/thoughtomics/did-life-evolve-in-a-warm-little-pond/#:~:text=Charles%20Darwin%20was%20reluctant%20to,of%20life%20could%20have%20formed.

[30] Sean Jordan, "Origins of Life: New Evidence First Cells Could Have Formed at the Bottom of the Ocean," *The Conversation,* November 7, 2019, https://theconversation.com/origins-of-life-new-evidence-first-cells-could-have-formed-at-the-bottom-of-the-ocean-126228.

Following that line of reasoning, if evolution *did not* occur, then how did the Lord create birds from the waters?

Although the Bible does not use the same in-depth terminology, the process of commanding life from the waters would imply an evolutionary state of creation, beginning with single-cell organisms in the water that progressively multiplied and divided into the evolution of all living things—just like the Bible's depiction of birds, whales, and "every living creature which moveth."

Please don't forget that the Trinity is the matrix, meaning that all of evolution existed as nothing more than the Trinity continuously interacting with Itself in ever-changing forms. However, it appears as if the only thing that is *not* the Trinity are the souls of all living creatures, which is what separates living creatures from inanimate objects.

What is a living soul created from?

Odds are that living souls are little more than something resembling the computer code that allows software to operate.

Enter the *gap theory*.

Traditional Christian theology has long contended our earth is about six thousand years old, having been made during the six twenty-four-hour days of creation. Then, as geological and fossilized evidence began to mount in favor of evolution, a gap theory of billions of years was formulated in order to defend the scriptures against evolution.

This theory states that a gap exists in Genesis chapter 1, between verses 1 and 2, of millions or billions of years through which a pre-Adamic race of people lived, as well as the timeframe in which Lucifer rebelled against God and was cast out of heaven onto the earth.

In his article for the Institute for Christian Research, Henry M. Morris, PhD, wrote,

> According to this concept, Genesis 1:1 describes the initial creation of the universe. Following this, the standard events of cosmic evolution took place, which eventually produced our solar system about five billion years ago. Then, on the earth, the various geologic ages followed, as identified by their respective assemblages of fossils (trilobites, dinosaurs, etc.).
>
> But then occurred a devastating global cataclysm, destroying all life on Earth and leaving a vast fossil graveyard everywhere. This situation is then said to be what is described in Genesis 1:2. "And the earth was without form and void; and darkness was upon the face of the deep." The cataclysm is thought to have occurred as a result of the rebellion of Satan and his angels against their Creator in Heaven, with God then casting them out of Heaven to the earth.
>
> Those who advocate the gap theory agree that the six days of the creation week were literal days, but they interpret them only as days of *recreation*, with God creating again many of the kinds of animals and plants destroyed in the cataclysm.

What is the purpose of the Gap Theory?

The gap theory was developed mainly for the purpose of accommodating the great ages demanded by evolutionary geologists. This idea was first popularized by a Scottish theologian, Thomas Chalmers, early in the 19th century. In this country, the famous *Scofield*

Study Bible made it an almost universally accepted teaching among fundamentalists.[31]

At the end of that gap period, a cataclysmic event, referred to as Lucifer's flood, utterly destroyed the Earth to the point that verse 2 reads, "And the earth without form, and void; and darkness was upon the face of the deep."

According to gap theorists, our prehistoric fossilized records are evidence, not of humankind's evolution, but rather of what God had originally created during that pre-Adamic gap. Meaning, those life-forms in the fossilized records didn't evolve but rather were originally created in their fossilized form.

Obviously, the greatest flaw in the gap theory is this:

If God created the heaven and the earth in verse 1, and billions of years later destroyed it to the extent that it was "without form, and void; and darkness was upon the face of the deep," thus ending that pre-Adamic gap, then those fossilized records would have been destroyed as well.

The second flaw in the gap theory is that it reads verse 2 as a chronological destruction of verse 1, instead of a new starting point in the story.

Think of it like this: "In the beginning God created the heaven and the earth" is like a chapter title, while "And the earth was without form, and void; and darkness was upon the face of the deep" becomes the first sentence of the story.

Meaning that planet Earth simply hadn't been created yet, as darkness currently filled the space where the earth would one day circle.

---

[31] Henry M. Morris, "Why the Gap Theory Won't Work," ICR, November 1, 1997, https://www.icr.org/article/why-gap-theory-wont-work/.

Unfortunately, the gap theory is a perfect example of the types of misinterpretations that can be made when one lacks a basic understanding of scientific principles.

Along with that, creationists and evolutionists differ in two other primary ways:

1. Traditional creationists believe that the six days of creation were literally six twenty-four-hour days, while evolutionists believe that the evolutionary process of life took billions of years through a series of stages.

   Evolutionists are correct.

   Creationists failed to realize that the six days of creation are figurative for stages of creation, with each stage existing in varying time frames; gap theorists sought ways to defend the scriptures against evolution, as opposed to revising their interpretations until the scriptures and scientific evidence came into agreement.

2. Evolutionists believe humankind was created through an evolutionary process that originally began in the waters as single-cell organisms, whereby anthropologists have long sought the missing link between man and Neanderthal.

   Creationists reject the evolution of humankind, as they contend humankind was created from the dust of the earth in accordance with the Genesis account of creation.

   Creationists are correct.

   However, in all fairness, both have failed to discern that life was created twice upon the earth, in two separate stages of development:

- first, *from the waters* on day five, through the theory of evolution;
- second, *from the earth* on day six, through the traditional creation account of Adam and Eve.

Our scientific community has correctly theorized that a meteor strike ended our prehistoric era (day five), through which evolution as we know it ceased, and then ushered in the era of man, with our more civilized animal and insect kingdoms (day six).

However, that meteor strike didn't immediately kill all prehistoric life. DNA evidence has proven an overlap between man and Neanderthal,[32] meaning anthropologists will *never* discover the missing link between man and Neanderthals simply because there isn't one.

Adam and Eve are, for lack of better wording, the missing link. Adam and Eve were created separately from our prehistoric and evolutionary life forms, meaning that evolution as we know it, through the theory of evolution, ceased with that meteor strike.

---

[32] Ker Than, "Neanderthals, Humans Interbred—First Solid DNA Evidence," *National Geographic*, May 8, 2010, https://www.nationalgeographic.com/news/2010/5/100506-science-neanderthals-humans-mated-interbred-dna-gene/.

DAY SIX

⁓

The Creation
of Man

If we do discover a complete theory, it should in time
be understandable in broad principle by everyone, not
just a few scientists. Then we shall all, philosophers,
scientists, and just ordinary people, be able to take
part in the discussion of the question of why it is
that we and the universe exist. If we find the answer
to that, it would be the ultimate triumph of human
reason—for then we would know the mind of God.

—Stephen Hawking

Day six, the re-creation of life.

And God said, *Let the earth bring forth* the living
creature after his kind, cattle, and creeping thing, and
beast of the earth after his kind: and it was so. And
God made the beast of the earth after his kind, and
cattle after their kind, and every thing that creepeth
upon the earth after his kind: and God saw that it was

good. And God said, Let us make man in our image, after our likeness: and let them have dominion over the fish of the sea, and over the fowl of the air, and over the cattle, and over all the earth, and over every creeping thing that creepeth upon the earth. So God created man in his own image, in the image of God created he him; male and female created he them. And God blessed them, and God said unto them, Be fruitful, and multiply, and *replenish the earth*, and subdue it: and have dominion over the fish of the sea, and over the fowl of the air, and over every living thing that moveth upon the earth. (Genesis 1:24–28, italics added)

Notice that:

On day five God said, "Let the waters bring forth."

Then later, on day six, He said, "Let the earth bring forth."

Next, consider the phrase *replenish the earth*, as the Oxford Learner's Dictionary defines replenish as: To make something full again by replacing what has been used.[33]

Using that definition of what the Lord said to Adam and Eve, now compare it with what He later said to Noah after the flood: "And God blessed Noah and his sons, and said unto them, Be fruitful and multiply, and *replenish the earth*" (Genesis 9:1, italics added).

In short, the Lord commanded Noah to replenish the earth after the flood just as He previously commanded Adam and Eve to replenish the earth after day five's prehistoric era had ended.

---

[33] Oxford Learner's Dictionaries, s.v. (verb), accessed December 28, 2020, https://www. oxfordlearnersdictionaries.com/us/definition/american_english/replenish#:~:text=to% 20make%20something%20full%20again,the%20Oxford%20Advanced%20Learner's%20 Dictionary.

Notice, humankind was also created in the image and likeness of God, which we'll now expound on.

The image of God means existing in three separate and distinct bodies: just as the Trinity exists as the Father, Son, and Holy Spirit, so also man exists with a soul, physical body, and spirit. In order to better understand this, consider the analogy of a three-part laptop computer:

1. Hardware is a laptop's tangible components:

    A. As is your physical body to you.
    B. As are, in some respects, elementary particles to mass.
    C. As is Jesus to the Trinity.

2. Software is a laptop's intangible components of "knowledge":

    A. As is your soul to you, being your will, intellect, and emotions, which make you distinct from everyone else, whereby sin acts as a type of virus that prevents the software of your soul from working properly.
    B. As is the light of the laws of knowledge to creation.
    C. As is God the Father to the Trinity.

3. Electricity is a laptop's life force:

    A. As is your spirit to you.
    B. As are the four known forces of nature to creation.
    C. As is the Holy Spirit to the Trinity.

The likeness of God means those three separate and distinct bodies perfectly interact together as one, just as any substance that exists in a three-in-one state of singularity, such as H_2O or the Trinity, exists in the mathematical formula of $1 \times 1 \times 1 = 1$.

Fortunately, Matthew 6:22 reveals to us what the likeness of God is, "The light of the body is the eye: if therefore thine eye be single, thy whole body shall be full of light"—just as the Trinity perfectly interacts together with Itself free of internal strife and division, being *one eye full of light with no darkness at all.*

With that said, when Adam and Eve were first created, so too were they in the image and likeness of God, being 1 x 1 x 1 = 1, as *one eye full of light with no darkness at all.*

However, that all changed when they chose to partake of the forbidden fruit, through which a type of spiritual virus entered into them in order to convert them from 1 x 1 x 1 = 1 into 1 + 1 + 1 = 3; or, as Matthew 6:23 reads, "But if thine eye be evil, thy whole body shall be full of darkness. If therefore the light that is in thee be darkness, how great is that darkness!"

They had fallen from the unified image and likeness of God, having been free of internal strife and division as *one eye full of light with no darkness at all,* and into their fallen state, full of internal strife and division as *an evil eye full of darkness.*

Unintentionally, through their newfound internal state of division, they planted within themselves the spiritual seeds of worry, anxiety, and depression, which in time would cloud their spiritual vision through their inner turmoil and strife. Throughout the remainder of their lives their spiritual desires would wage war against their fleshly desires, and thus force their souls to referee between the two.

Thankfully, that's where our born-again experience comes into play, for just as Samson's physical strength was restored to him when his hair grew back, so too is our spiritual strength restored to us through our acceptance of Christ, That in turn converts us back into a dim light state of 1 x 1 x 1 = 1, in which we're allowed to continuously grow into ever brighter levels.

However, contrary to the teachings of some, being made in the image and likeness of God does not mean that humankind shares all His attributes. For instance, one famous televangelist loves to brag that being made in the image and likeness of God allows the words that man speaks to have the same creative power as God's words do, meaning we can "Name it and claim it" and "Blab it and grab it" as we speak our desires into existence.

Which is stupid.

God the Father, as the light of the laws of knowledge, can speak things into existence only because the Trinity and the universe are one, as elementary particles (the Son) and the four fundamental forces of nature (the Holy Spirit) always do the will of the laws of knowledge—always!

Conversely, the words that man speaks do not contain the same creative power as the Lord's because humankind is not one with the universe. Granted, we're a small part that is connected with the universe, but that isn't the same as being one with it.

Next, evolutionists have long contended that humankind evolved from Neanderthals due to our common DNA, even though the evolution of man is definitely contrary to scripture; as such, our common DNA most probably came from at least one or two other sources.

The first potential source is found in Genesis 2:7 (italics added): "And the Lord God formed man of *the dust* of the ground, and breathed into his nostrils the breath of life; and man became a living soul."

What is the *dust of the ground*?

Astrophysicist Karel Schrijver stated,

When stars get to the end of their lives, they swell up and fall together again, throwing off their outer layers. If a star is heavy enough, it will explode in a supernova.

So most of the material that we're made of comes out of dying stars, or stars that died in explosions. And those stellar explosions continue. We have stuff in us as old as the universe, and then some stuff that landed here maybe only a hundred years ago. And all of that mixes in our bodies.[34]

Supernovas dust nearby planetary bodies with their mineral remnants, which means that our physical bodies are comprised of supernova residues, in such forms as iron, zinc, copper, and magnesium, which had previously dusted the earth's surface.

Along with that, DNA from primates and Neanderthals also existed within our soil as well; ergo, humankind was created from the dust of the earth that contained supernova mineral remnants, as well as primate and Neanderthal DNA.

A second potential source might also be found in sexual sin, for though we're never told what the fruit from the tree of the knowledge of good and evil actually was, traditional Christian theology believes it to have been a literal piece of fruit, such as an apple from an apple tree—though I highly doubt it.

There are too many other figurative verses in Genesis for us to suddenly believe that the tree of life and the tree of the knowledge of good and evil were both literally trees. As previously mentioned,

---

[34] Simon Worral, "How 40,000 Tons of Cosmic Dust Falling to Earth Affects You and Me," *National Geographic*, January 28, 2015, https://www.nationalgeographic.com/news/2015/01/150128-big-bang-universe-supernova-astrophysics-health-space-ngbooktalk/#close.

I'm highly confident those two trees were symbolic for obedience, but how?

Because DNA evidence has proven an overlap between man and Neanderthal, as not all Neanderthals were immediately killed by that meteor strike, then it seems more probable than not that those two trees were symbolic for sexual relations with the remaining Neanderthals.

As such, to obediently refrain from carnal relations with those Neanderthals would be a tree of life to Adam and Eve, through which types of blessings would ensue. Conversely, to disobediently engage in carnal sins would be a tree of the knowledge of good and evil to them, through which types of curses would ensue.

With that said, for *National Geographic*, Ker Than wrote,

> According to a new DNA study, most humans have a little Neanderthal in them—at least 1 to 4 percent of a person's genetic makeup.
>
> The study uncovered the first solid genetic evidence that "modern" humans—or Homo sapiens—interbred with their Neanderthal neighbors, who mysteriously died out about 30,000 years ago.[35]

This means that humankind's common DNA with Neanderthals wasn't necessarily the result of humankind's evolution from Neanderthals but rather was a result of cohabitation that might have begun as Adam and Eve's original sin, and/or their offspring's sin as well.

Regardless, at the end of day six, Genesis 2:2 reads, "And on the seventh day God ended his work which he had made; and he rested on the seventh day from all his work which he had made."

---

[35] Than, "Neanderthals, Humans Interbred."

God's rest ended day six of creation and in turn began day seven, in which we currently live. Subsequently, day seven will end, and in turn day eight will begin, with the second coming of Christ per Matthew 24:29–31 (italics added):

> *Immediately after the tribulation* of those days shall the sun be darkened, and the moon shall not give her light, and the stars shall fall from heaven, and the powers of the heavens shall be shaken: And *then shall appear the sign* of the Son of man in heaven: and then shall all the tribes of the earth mourn, and they shall see the Son of man coming in the clouds of heaven with power and great glory. And he shall send his angels with a great sound of a trumpet, and *they shall gather together his elect* from the four winds, from one end of heaven to the other.

This in turn reveals that the pretribulation rapture, which has been so prominently proclaimed by countless ministers and televangelists, is in error, as this verse plainly reads in a series of clean-cut stages:

1. *"Immediately after the tribulation of those days,"* meaning the Great Tribulation.
2. "And *then shall appear the sign* of the Son of man in heaven," meaning His second coming.
3. "And he shall send his angels with a great sound of a trumpet, and *they shall gather together his elect* from the four winds, from one end of heaven to the other," which is the rapture of the church.

Notice, "immediately after" is *not* synonymous with "immediately before"; in fact, it's the antithesis!

It doesn't get much clearer than that, as the rapture will most definitely occur at the end of the Great Tribulation, and not before, which is contrary to many of today's most popular end-time messages.

After day six of creation was completed, Genesis 2:1–2 states, "Thus the heavens and the earth were finished, and all the host of them. And on the seventh day God ended his work which he had made; and he rested on the seventh day from all his work which he had made."

As God the Father is still at rest from His prior six days of work, humankind still exists in day seven of creation, which will not end until Christ returns for His bride, His church, when day eight will finally begin.

I will now close with these words from Neil deGrasse Tyson:

> Recognize that the very molecules that make up your body, the atoms that construct the molecules, are traceable to the crucibles that were once the centers of high mass stars that exploded their chemically rich guts into the galaxy, enriching pristine gas clouds with the chemistry of life. So that we are all connected to each other biologically, to the earth chemically and to the rest of the universe atomically. That's kinda cool! That makes me smile and I actually feel quite large at the end of that. It's not that we are better than the universe, we are part of the universe. We are in the universe and the universe is in us.[36]

---

[36] The History Channel, "*The Universe*, S1E14 'Beyond the Big Bang,'" March 8, 2017, YouTube video, 1:28:22, https://www.youtube.com/watch?v=OkwO8Kq8RIU

Printed in the United States
by Baker & Taylor Publisher Services